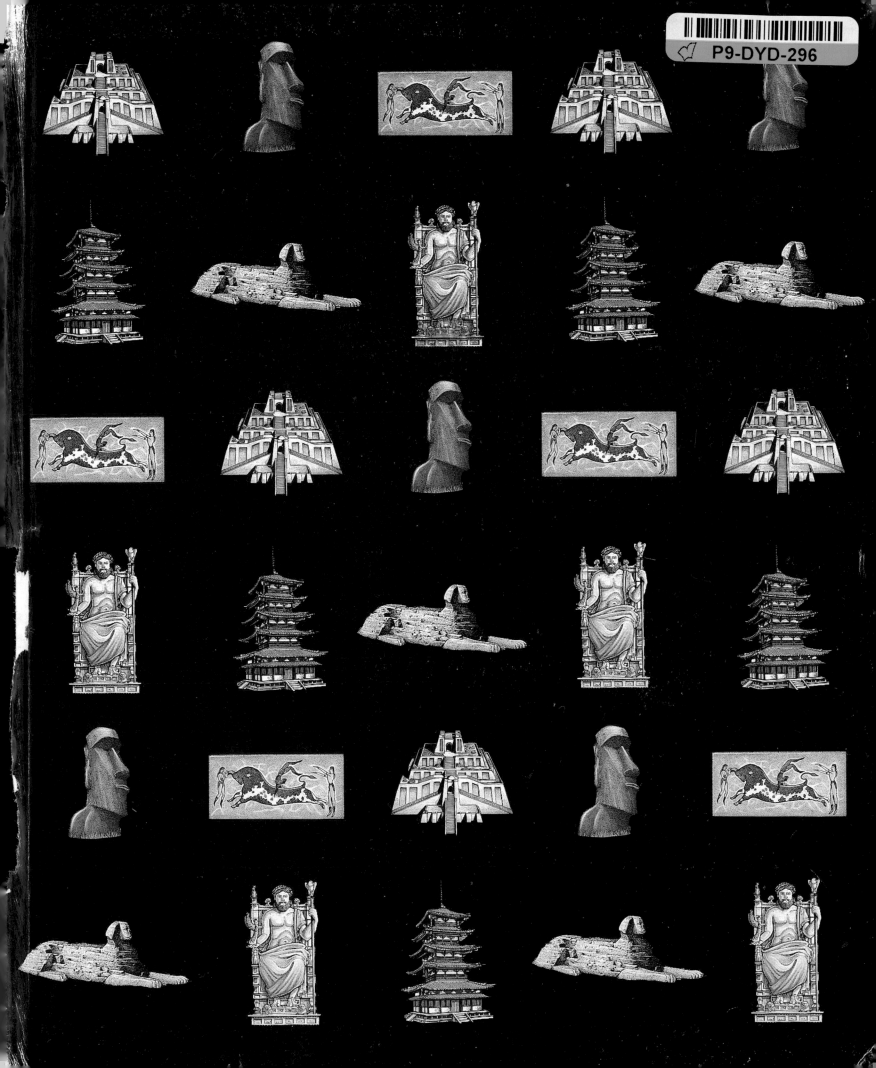

ANCIENT
WONDERS

TIM WOOD

VIKING

Acknowledgments

The publishers would like to thank Bill Donohoe and Jonathan Adams, who illustrated the see-through scenes; James Field, who illustrated the cover; and the individuals and organizations that have given their permission to reproduce the following pictures:

Ancient Art & Architecture Collection: 11 bottom right, 15 bottom right, 18 top left, 23 top right, 26 top right, 33 bottom right, 38 center left, 45 bottom right.
Bruce Coleman Ltd: /Herbert Kranawetter 33 top right.
C. M. Dixon: 4 top left, 6 top left, 7 top right, 7 bottom center, 10 top left, 16 top left, 19 top left, 26 top left, 27 top right, 28 top left, 31 top right, 41 bottom right.
e.t. archive: 22 top left.
Mansell Collection: 15 center, 19 top right.
Peter Clayton: 21 top left, 29 top right.
Planet Earth Pictures: 5 bottom right, 39 bottom right.
Magnum: /F. Mayer 24 center, /Cornel Capa 34 top right, /Harry Gruyaert 36 top right, /B. Barbey 43 bottom right.
Robert Estall Photo Library: 12 top right.
Robert Harding Picture Library: /Rolf Richardson 25 center, 42 top right.
Sonia Halliday: 22 top right.
Tony Stone Images: /Tom Till 37 top.
Werner Forman Archive: /Ohio State Museum 35 bottom left, /Museum of the American Indian, Heye Foundation, New York 35 bottom right, 42 top left, 44 top right.
ZEFA: /K. Kerth 30 top left, 32 top left.

Illustrators:
Jonathan Adams: icons, 15, 21, 28 middle, 44–45. **James Field (Simon Girling):** cover.
Terry Gabbey (Associated Freelance Artists): 10–11, 12–13, 20, 30, 31, 36, 38, 39.
Richard Hook: 46–47. **Bill Le Fever:** 18–19, 22–23, 32–33, 42. **Kevin Madison:** 5, 37.
Angus McBride (Linden Artists): title page, 4, 6, 7, 14, 26, 27, 28–29, 34, 43.

VIKING
Published by the Penguin Group
Penguin Books USA Inc., 375 Hudson Street, New York, New York 10014, U.S.A.
Penguin Books Ltd, 27 Wrights Lane, London W8 5TZ, England
Penguin Books Australia Ltd, Ringwood, Victoria, Australia
Penguin Books Canada Ltd, 10 Alcorn Avenue, Toronto, Ontario, Canada M4V 3B2
Penguin Books (N.Z.) Ltd, 182–190 Wairau Road, Auckland 10, New Zealand

Penguin Books Ltd, Registered Offices: Harmondsworth, Middlesex, England

First published in Great Britain by Heinemann Children's Reference,
a division of Reed Educational & Professional Publishing Ltd., 1997
First published in the United States of America by Viking,
a division of Penguin Books USA Inc., 1997

1 3 5 7 9 10 8 6 4 2

Copyright © Reed Educational & Professional Publishing Ltd., 1997

Library of Congress Catalog Card Number: 96-61598

ISBN 0-670-87468-X

Printed in Italy

CONTENTS

Wonders of the World 4
Ziggurats for the Gods 6
Egyptian Royal Tombs 8
Pyramids and Sphinx 10
Stone Circles 12
City of Troy 14
Palace of Knossos 16
Gardens of Babylon 18
Alexandria 20
Solomon's Temple 22
Petra—City of Rock 24
Zeus at Olympia 26
Harbor at Carthage 28
The Seven Wonders 30
Roman Wonders 32
American Wonders 34
Easter Island Statues 36
Chichén Itzá 38
Hagia Sophia 40
Borobudur 42
Wonders at Nara 44
Key Dates and Glossary 46
Index 48

WONDERS OF THE WORLD

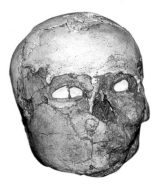

This skull was found at Jericho. It has been decorated with clay and shells to imitate the dead person's features.

Jericho was probably the oldest walled settlement in the world. The city became rich through trading salt, and the inhabitants built walls to protect themselves and their wealth. They used mud bricks, made by hand and dried in the sun.

Two thousand years ago, ancient Greek and Roman tourists visited the world's greatest sites just as tourists do today. Ancient writers picked out the most spectacular sites and called them the Seven Wonders of the World. Many other wonders were not included in this list because they had already disappeared or were not yet built when the list was compiled. This book includes some of these other sites and monuments.

Unfortunately, many have been destroyed over time, but the work of archaeologists and historians has helped to reconstruct many of them.

THE FIRST SETTLEMENTS

The first humans were nomadic hunters and scavengers. It was not until humans learned to farm the land that they began to live in one place. They did this to cultivate their land and to guard their crops. Realizing there was strength in numbers, humans gathered in groups and established settlements and communities.

Perhaps the earliest ancient wonder was the city of Jericho. It was probably the first walled settlement in the world, dating from about 8000 B.C. The people of Jericho built a high wall around the city to protect themselves and their wealth. These walls were some of the earliest known defenses built anywhere in the world.

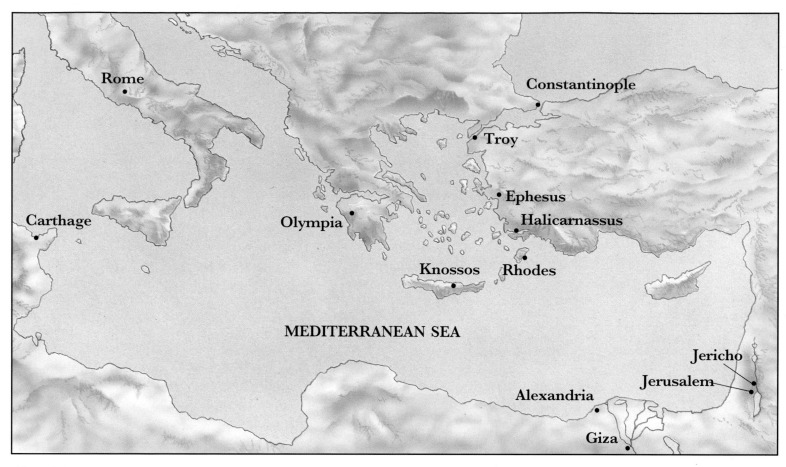

Rome •

Constantinople •

Troy •

Ephesus •
Halicarnassus •

Carthage •

Olympia •

Knossos •
Rhodes •

MEDITERRANEAN SEA

Jericho •
Jerusalem •

Alexandria •

Giza •

Many of the most famous wonders were built by the ancient Egyptians, Greeks, and Romans. The large map shows where they were built. The smaller map shows other ancient wonders featured in this book, located in different parts of the world.

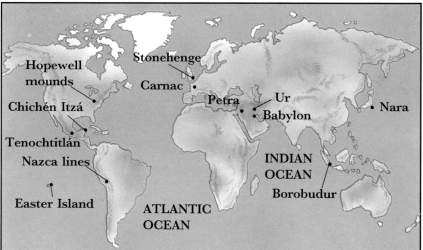

Hopewell mounds •

Stonehenge •
Carnac •

Ur •
Petra • Babylon •

Nara •

Chichén Itzá •

Tenochtitlán •

Nazca lines •

INDIAN OCEAN

Borobudur •

Easter Island •

ATLANTIC OCEAN

WHY BUILD WONDERS?

Many rulers ordered the creation of monuments and buildings. These were usually intended to show the rulers' power, to fill their subjects with awe, and to strike fear into the hearts of their enemies. Priests wanted bigger and better temples to show that their gods were more powerful than the gods in other lands. The people helped to build these monuments and temples because they believed it would impress the gods who protected and fed them.

ANCIENT SIGHTSEEING

These monuments inspired craftworkers to create more beautiful decorations to adorn bigger and better palaces and temples. They learned how to make more lifelike statues and invented ways of coloring bricks and tiles. Soon people began traveling to see the spectacular sights—the wonders of the world.

A formation of salt found in the Dead Sea. Salt was important in the ancient world for preserving food. It was quite easy for the people of Jericho to collect salt from the Dead Sea and trade it with other people. This helped the city become rich.

5

ZIGGURATS FOR THE GODS

This golden helmet, which may have belonged to a king, was found with a golden dagger in the city of Ur. It is shaped like a man's head with the hair drawn into a bun at the back.

The ziggurat of Ur, in Mesopotamia, was built about 2100 B.C. Made entirely of mud bricks, ziggurats were built in the shape of flattened pyramids with outside staircases, and were found in most cities in Mesopotamia (now modern Iraq). Most were crowned with a temple or shrine where priests worshipped the gods of each city.

LAND BETWEEN THE RIVERS

Mesopotamia means "land between the rivers." The area was watered by two mighty rivers, the Tigris and the Euphrates, which created a fertile plain between the two. The first inhabitants built complicated systems of ditches and canals in order to irrigate the land for farming. As the Mesopotamians became more organized, they built cities along the riverbanks. Each city had its own king and its own gods to worship.

MESOPOTAMIAN GODS

The Mesopotamians worshipped gods representing the powerful forces of nature that shaped their lives. Among them were An, the sky god, who provided life-giving rain, and Enlil, the wind god.

The gods were worshipped in vast sacred temple enclosures built within each city. Each enclosure contained a ziggurat, usually crowned with a temple or shrine where the main worship took place.

Priests preparing a meal for the gods at the ziggurat of Ur. The largest ziggurats were nearly 90,000 square feet and 150 feet high. Most ziggurats and other large buildings in Mesopotamia were built by slaves.

Originally a Mesopotamian scribe drew pictures by pressing a pointed stick into wet clay. Over time this method of drawing became writing made of wedge-shaped marks.

Each city in Mesopotamia had its own king. They often fought each other over precious water and to seize treasure. Scribes would keep a record of this wealth using wedge-shaped marks on clay tablets—the first forms of writing.

ZIGGURATS

The earliest ziggurat was built at Eridu in about 5000 B.C. Ziggurats were solid structures with no rooms inside them. It is uncertain why they were shaped the way they were, but it seems likely that the Mesopotamians thought of them as altars or, perhaps, as stairways to and for the gods. Built by slaves, the largest ziggurats were over 150 feet high.

LOOKING AFTER THE GODS

The priests wanted their gods to keep living in their city. To do this, they encouraged the citizens to pray and bring offerings of food. We know that in the city of Uruk, the gods required daily offerings of 250 loaves, over 1,000 date cakes, 50 sheep, eight lambs, two oxen, and a calf!

The gods also "owned" lands that were governed for them by the priests. Priests collected taxes and invented a form of writing to keep track of the gods' wealth. Called "cuneiform," the writing consisted of wedge-shaped marks made in clay tablets. Thousands of examples survive today.

MUD BRICKS

Since there was very little natural building stone in Mesopotamia, ziggurats were built almost entirely of mud bricks made of dirt mixed with water and chopped straw. The mixture was poured into wooden molds and either left to dry and harden in the sun or baked in kilns. Some bricks were covered with a tarlike substance called bitumen to make them waterproof. Thousands of years later, worn down by the weather, the bricks have crumbled. Little now remains of the great buildings of Mesopotamia except mounds of dried earth.

Some kings of Mesopotamia became incredibly rich through conquest. They owned wonderful objects, such as this lyre decorated with a golden bull's head. Mesopotamian kings and queens were buried with their favorite possessions. Fabulous gold, silver, and bronze treasures have been found at the royal tombs at Ur.

EGYPTIAN ROYAL TOMBS

The see-through scene on this page shows the Great Pyramid at Giza during its construction. On this page, builders are moving blocks of stone up a continuous ramp using ropes and wooden rollers. When the page is turned, the pyramid is almost complete. Builders are adding the polished limestone slabs that covered its surface. In the background, other builders are leveling an area for a pyramid for one of the wives of the pharaoh. A series of channels are filled with water and then the site is leveled to the water's surface.

The most famous pyramid (Egyptian royal tomb) is the Great Pyramid at Giza, in Egypt. It is the tomb of Pharaoh Cheops. Work began in about 2550 B.C., and it took thousands of workers about 20 years to finish.

THE GREAT PYRAMID

This structure cost 1,600 silver talents to build—over $7.5 million in today's values. It is made from 2,300,000 blocks of yellow limestone, each weighing at least 2.75 tons. It was originally 480 feet high and, until the late 19th century, was the tallest manmade structure in the world.

CUTTING THE BLOCKS

We know the stone for the pyramids came from quarries on the opposite bank of the Nile river. The giant blocks were split from the surrounding rock using wooden wedges. These were driven into cracks in the rocks and then soaked in water. As the wood swelled, it split the stones neatly. The marks of this work can still be seen in the old quarries.

Copper chisels and stone hammers were used to smooth the stones. The blocks were brought from the quarries on boats, then dragged along a causeway from the river to the pyramid site using wooden rollers or sledges.

1 Pharaoh's burial chamber
2 Airshafts that ventilate chamber
3 Stones used to seal entrance to chamber
4 Incomplete burial chambers
5 Exit shafts for workmen
6 Limestone slabs covering surface

MOVING THE STONES

Some archaeologists believe the stones were dragged up giant ramps into their final positions. There might have been several ramps or a continuous ramp that went around the pyramid like the one shown on the see-through scene (left). However, ramps on this scale would have required nearly three times as much building material as the pyramids themselves. We do not know what happened to this material when the pyramids were finished.

A SHINING MONUMENT

When built, the surface of the Great Pyramid was covered with polished limestone slabs. Finally the tip was crowned with a golden cap.

7 Central pyramid
8 Bedrock to level slope
9 Ramp
10 Colonnaded walkways
11 Underground passage
12 Pharaoh's burial chamber

DEIR EL BAHRI

The see-through scene below shows another impressive royal tomb—that of Pharaoh Mentuhotpe I, at Deir el Bahri. It combines a mortuary (death) temple and pyramid to make a single building carved out of a solid cliff face. It was finished about 2010 B.C., over 500 years after the last of the pyramids was built at Giza. All royal tombs had causeways. The causeway to Mentuhotpe's temple was 150 feet wide. There was also a wide ramp leading up to the temple. The central pyramid was surrounded by large terraces supported on colonnaded walkways. The roof of the largest terrace was supported by 140 columns. The pharaoh's body was placed in a chamber cut into the cliff face, reached only by an underground passage.

Over 500 years after the last pyramid was completed at Giza, the royal tomb on this page was built at Deir el Bahri. It was for Pharaoh Mentuhotpe I. Rows of trees were planted at the front of the tomb, and it was approached by a causeway and a wide ramp. When the see-through page is turned, the inside of the temple is shown, including the central pyramid and the burial chamber carved out of the solid cliff face. This chamber was reached by an underground passage nearly 500 feet long.

PYRAMIDS AND SPHINX

A gold pendant from the tomb of Tutankhamun. Treasure attracted tomb robbers who, in spite of the presence of guards, stripped the royal tombs bare.

Historians like Herodotus used to believe that the pyramids were built by slaves. In reality, the Egyptians did the work willingly. When the annual flooding of the Nile occurred, the farmers had little else to do. Some worked on the pyramids instead of paying taxes. Since the Egyptians believed their pharaoh (the Egyptian king) was a god, building a pyramid would have been an important act of worship.

The Egyptians believed the pharaoh was a god, so he was buried in great splendor, and his body was embalmed to preserve it. The coffin was carried in a funeral procession to a boat, where it was transported along the sacred Nile river.

Cheops came to the throne and plunged into all manner of wickedness. He closed the temples and forced the Egyptians to work in his service. Some were required to drag blocks of stone down to the Nile from quarries.

— *Herodotus* —

ROYAL TOMBS

Priests performed sacred ceremonies associated with the dead pharaohs in temples built around the base of the pyramids. Around the site at Giza, smaller tombs and pyramids were built to house the bodies of members of the royal family. Causeways connected the mortuary temples to the Nile so the funeral procession could pass with ease from the river to the temple.

The passages and burial rooms under the pyramid were built first. Artists began decorating the walls with carvings and paintings while the rooms were still open to daylight, and finished working by torchlight once the roof was completed.

ROYAL FUNERAL

The Egyptians believed the pyramids were places where the dead traveled to a new life. When a pharaoh died, many of his most valuable possessions were buried with him. However, this buried wealth attracted thieves who broke in and stole many of the treasures. Eventually, the Egyptians stopped building pyramids and buried their pharaohs in a steep-sided valley, "The Valley of the Kings," which they mistakenly believed would be easier to guard.

THE GREAT SPHINX

Close to the pyramids at Giza lies one of the greatest mysteries of ancient Egypt, the Great Sphinx. This colossal figure of a lion with the head of a man—possibly the Pharaoh Khephren—is 240 feet long and 65 feet high. The figure is carved from a huge limestone rock and was, at times in its long history, covered with shaped and carved stones, or buried up to its neck in sand. No one is sure when or why it was built. Perhaps this mysterious creature is simply the guardian of the pyramids.

The picture at right shows the royal coffin, or sarcophagus, that belonged to Tutankhamun—the only pharaoh whose tomb has been found intact in the Valley of the Kings.

The cutaways (below) show the network of corridors and chambers inside the three pyramids at Giza. They also show the passages and burial rooms under the pyramids.

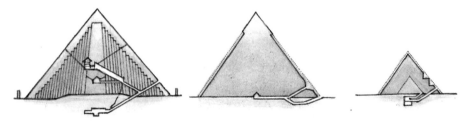

Great Pyramid of Cheops   **Pyramid of Khephren**   **Pyramid of Menkaure**

11

STONE CIRCLES

The spectacular avenues of menhirs at Carnac point roughly from east to west. Was it a graveyard or a Stone Age computer used for predicting the movement of the sun or stars? We may never know.

Megalithic monuments were built by the early farming settlements in Europe about **6,000** years ago. The earliest monuments were tombs; however, the exact purpose of many of the structures built after **3200** B.C. has been lost to us.

STONE AGE MEGALITHS

Early Stone Age monuments are known as megaliths, from "mega," meaning "big," and "lith," meaning "stone." Some monuments are single standing stones, known as "menhirs." "Dolmens" are structures made up of several stones.

THE AVENUES OF CARNAC

One of the largest megaliths is located in western France, near the village of Carnac. This monument contains over 3,000 prehistoric menhirs and dolmens. Some of the stones are colossal—up to 20 feet high. They are arranged in organized groups that form long avenues of upright stones. Some avenues contain as many as 13 rows of stones and are up to 330 feet wide. The avenues stretch for two and a half miles. Among the lines of menhirs are stone altars, stone circles, and megalithic tombs.

SUN AND STARS

The monument, which was started in about 3000 B.C., was built over a period of 1,000 years. We do not know why it was built or who built it. Archaeologists have suggested that each stone represents a dead ancestor, or that the stones were used to measure the movement of the sun or stars.

STONEHENGE

Some megalithic monuments are arranged in rows or circular ditched enclosures known as "henges." There are over 1,000 stone circles and 80 henges in Britain. The largest, Stonehenge, was used as a ceremonial or religious center from about 3300 B.C.

HUMAN SACRIFICE?

The first builders surrounded the site with a circular ditch and bank. Inside the ditch is a ring of 56 smaller pits, named Aubrey holes after John Aubrey, their 17th-century discoverer. The holes were used for the burial of cremated bodies—perhaps victims of human sacrifice. Outside the entrance, builders put up a huge menhir called the Heelstone and a timber gate.

THE STONE CIRCLE

About 2800 B.C., people of the Beaker Culture built a track, the "Avenue," to the entrance. A double circle of menhirs was built inside the earlier ring. The menhirs came from the Preseli Mountains in southwestern Wales, over 130 miles away. They were probably dragged part of the way and then carried on rafts—a task involving thousands of workers! About 2000 B.C., a circle of 30 upright stones was added. A horseshoe-shaped formation of five dolmens was built inside this circle.

GIANT CALENDAR

The size and careful design of Stonehenge indicate that it must have been an important site. An imaginary line drawn through the double circle and down the Avenue points to the position of the rising sun at the summer solstice. To some historians this suggests that Stonehenge was connected with sun worship. Other historians believe it was a giant Stone Age computer for predicting the movement of the sun and stars. The site is now so ruined that we will probably never know the real reason it was built.

The huge stones at Stonehenge could have been moved with the aid of ropes and rollers. The arrangement of ropes shown here might have been used to tip them upright.

Many megalithic monuments, including Stonehenge, may have been observatories for plotting the movements of the sun or stars. The ability to predict the seasons must have been very important to ancient peoples, whose lives depended heavily upon agriculture.

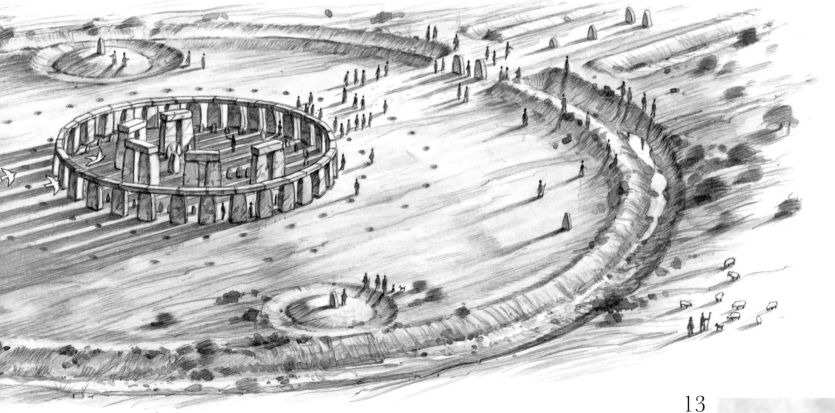

CITY OF TROY

The legend of ancient Troy is a wonderful story of a kidnapped queen, battles between famous heroes, and struggles between the gods, ending with one of the most cunning tricks ever played. For centuries scholars thought this was simply fiction created by the blind Greek poet Homer. One man, Heinrich Schliemann, made it his life's work to prove that Troy and all its wonders really did exist.

THE LEGEND OF TROY

The city and legend of Troy were described by the ancient Greek writer Homer over 3,000 years ago in his long poem, the *Iliad*. The poem tells how the beautiful Queen Helen was kidnapped by the Trojan prince, Paris.

It is not known whether the Trojan horse really existed or what it looked like. According to legend, the horse must have been huge, because part of the gateway had to be demolished to get it into Troy.

> Nine, then, is the number of years that we shall have to fight at Troy, and in the tenth its broad streets will be ours. Soldiers and fellow-countrymen, I call upon you to stand your ground till we capture Priam's spacious town.
>
> — *Homer, the* Iliad

Helen's husband, Menelaus, and his brother, King Agamemnon, raised a Greek army to attack Troy and rescue Helen. For ten years, the war raged. Homer describes great deeds of courage performed by heroes such as Hector and Achilles. Finally, Odysseus, king of Ithaca, came up with a clever plan that would fool the Trojans and allow the Greeks to capture the city of Troy.

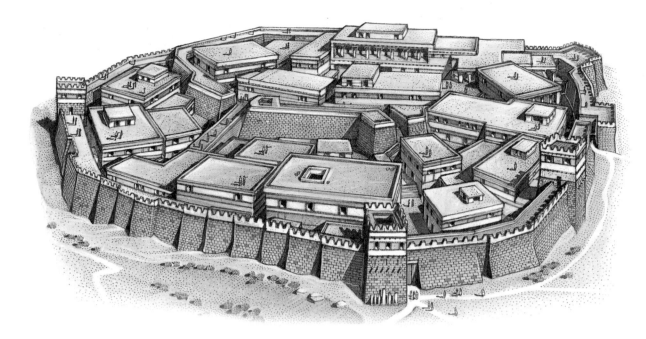

One of the surprising things about the remains of Troy is just how small the city was. It measured only 450 by 600 feet. This would have left space for no more than a few dozen houses for 1,000 people to live in! Perhaps only the rulers lived in the center of the city while the other citizens lived in wooden houses built outside the main stone citadel.

THE WOODEN HORSE

The Greeks built a huge wooden horse. They then pretended to sail away in defeat. The Trojans dragged the horse as a trophy into their city. But while the Trojans feasted in celebration of their victory, Greek soldiers who had hidden inside the horse crept out and opened the city gates. The Greek army, which had returned under cover of darkness, then destroyed the city.

Mrs. Schliemann wearing a gold diadem and necklace from Troy. Schliemann was so sure Hisarlik was Troy that he may have falsified some evidence to prove this.

SCHLIEMANN'S TROY

Homer, who was writing many years after the Trojan War, described Troy as being a stronghold on a hill with tall towers and a high wall.

In 1870, some scholars concluded that Troy could have stood on a great mound called Hisarlik in Turkey. Heinrich Schliemann, a rich German businessman and amateur archaeologist, decided to test the theory. Schliemann excavated the site from 1870 to 1890. Archaeologists now believe that Schliemann may have destroyed a lot of important evidence by his inexperience.

THE TREASURES OF TROY

Schliemann and later archaeologists claim to have discovered not one Troy, but nine! Each city was built on top of an earlier one. Some of the cities had been destroyed by fire, and one possibly by an earthquake. To this day, archaeologists are not sure which city was the Troy described by Homer. However, they know that the first settlers arrived there about 3000 B.C. Until about 1100 B.C., Troy was a fortress, and then a city until the last city of Troy fell in ruins about A.D. 400.

Among the ruins at Hisarlik, Schliemann discovered treasures made of gold, ivory, and jewels. Some of the treasures seemed too wonderful to be true, and Schliemann was accused of planting the treasure himself. Today, no one knows whether he really discovered the treasure of Priam, King of Troy.

A Greek vase, decorated with a scene from the Iliad, showing soldiers engaged in hand-to-hand combat. But did the Greeks and Trojans really fight a great war? The remains of Greek arrowheads and other weapons in the ruins suggest that the city might have been attacked by the Greeks. Some historians believe the "earthquake" damage that destroyed one city may have been caused by determined besiegers damaging the walls.

PALACE OF KNOSSOS

This statue of a snake goddess was found at Knossos. She holds two snakes, one in either hand, and may have been worshipped as part of a religion honoring nature.

The first European civilization developed on the island of Crete about **4,000** years ago. The kings of Crete became very wealthy through trade and used their wealth to build massive palaces. Knossos was the largest palace. It was home to King Minos and, according to legend, the Minotaur, a creature who was half man, half bull, and lived in the center of a labyrinth near the palace.

1 Bull-leaping in courtyard
2 King's chambers
3 Hall of pillars
4 Wall paintings
5 Storerooms
6 Workshops
7 Library

MINOAN PALACES

During the early Bronze Age, Cretan ships dominated trade between Africa, Asia, and Europe. Much of the trade passed through Crete, and the Cretan kings built huge palaces in which to store the trade goods. These palaces became distribution centers supplying food and luxuries to the people of Crete. The palaces were also the homes of craftworkers who made delicate pottery, worked precious metals, produced stone and crystal bowls, and carved gems.

KING MINOS

According to legend, the palace at Knossos was built by King Minos, the greatest of all the Cretan kings. However, King Minos may have been a mythical character, or the name may have been a common title used by all Cretan kings.

KNOSSOS

The royal apartments were richly decorated with wall paintings. Much of the ground floor was reserved for storerooms filled with stone-lined boxes and giant stone jars called "pithoi" that held grain, wine, and olive oil. Stone tablets on which the palace accounts were recorded suggest that over 4,000 people received rations from these stores.

BULL WORSHIP

The palace was also the center of rituals and religious ceremonies. Bull-leaping may have been performed in the courtyards at Knossos as part of these rituals. Cretan bull worship may have been similar to the ancient Greeks' worship of Poseidon, the god of the sea. Poseidon was seen as a bull whose hooves made the earth shake. The Cretans had good reason to fear an earth-shaking god because, in about 1700 B.C., an earthquake badly damaged the palaces in Crete. In 1450 B.C., a volcano on the island of Thera, about 60 miles away, erupted. Ash buried the palace at Knossos and tidal waves sank many Cretan ships, bringing the power of Crete to an end.

At the height of Minoan power, the palace of Knossos was five stories high and contained over 1,300 rooms. When the see-through page is turned, the inside of many of these rooms can be seen. The palace's walls were covered with painted scenes, including the bull-leaping wall painting shown on page 16 (top right). Bulls were worshipped by the Minoans, and bull-leaping took place in the courtyards at Knossos, with young men and women performing spectacular gymnastic leaps.

＝

GARDENS OF BABYLON

This stone tablet contains some of the earliest laws collected by King Hammurabi, who ruled Babylon from 1792 to 1750 B.C. Many of these, such as "an eye for an eye and a tooth for a tooth," later appeared in the Old Testament of the Christian Bible.

The Babylonians were skillful farmers who knew how to terrace and irrigate farmland. The Hanging Gardens might have been a series of irrigated terraces in the city, with trees and other plants growing on each level.

Babylon (from the word *Bab-ili*, meaning "Gate of God") has existed for nearly 4,500 years. Originally just a single city in Mesopotamia, Babylon became the center of a great empire. Conquered several times, it rose repeatedly from its own ashes to become great again. At the height of its power, Babylon was the legendary home of one of the Seven Wonders of the Ancient World—the Hanging Gardens.

THE HANGING GARDENS
According to legend, Nebuchadnezzar II, who ruled Babylon from 605 to 562 B.C., built the Hanging Gardens close to his palace for his wife Amitiya, daughter of the King of the Medes. Amitiya was homesick for her mountainous homeland, so the king built the fabulous gardens to remind her of home.

The gardens were believed to be like a giant ziggurat whose levels were constantly watered from the Euphrates river. Water trickled along channels to the plants, and greenery cascaded over the sides. Unfortunately, there is no convincing evidence to prove that the Hanging Gardens actually did exist. Babylon was surrounded by huge irrigation systems designed to make the land around the city bloom. Perhaps exaggerated stories told by awestruck visitors about these systems gradually grew into the legend of the gardens.

OTHER WONDERS
Babylon was one of the largest cities in the world at the time and was encircled by gigantic triple walls. The walls—second in length only to the Great Wall of China—were built of mud bricks waterproofed with bitumen, and stood nearly 90 feet high. Each wall surrounded the city, covering about 11 miles around the perimeter. The walls were decorated with multicolored glazed bricks and tiles and, according to legend, were wide enough for two chariots to race side by side along the top. They were pierced by huge gateways and defended by enormous square towers almost 100 feet high.

An estimated 575 dragons and young bulls made in glazed brick decorated the Ishtar Gate. Some of the walls were decorated with enameled lions (see page 18 top right).

The city and the tower, which the children of men builded is called Babel; because the Lord did there confound the language of all the earth; and from thence did the Lord scatter them abroad upon the face of all the earth.

—— *Genesis 11* ——

TOWER OF BABEL

The city was divided into two parts, one on either side of the Euphrates river. On the eastern bank was the old city. Over it towered a seven-tiered ziggurat—the Temple of Marduk. Marduk was the Babylonian god of the city. This huge structure may be what the Bible describes as the "Tower of Babel."

In the Bible, the Tower of Babel explains the origin of different languages. According to Genesis, the Babylonians

were a proud people who wanted to build a tower that reached the heavens. God decided to punish them for their vanity. He confused their language so none of the workers could understand each other, then scattered them around the world. The tower was never completed.

ISHTAR GATE

A road paved with limestone led northward from the Temple of Marduk. The walls along the road were decorated with animals in glazed and bas-relief brickwork. The route led through the Ishtar Gate, named after the Babylonian goddess of love. This gateway was 50 feet high and decorated with blue glazed bricks. Giant bulls—the symbols of Adad the lightning god—dragons—the symbols of Marduk—and fierce lions were prominent among the decorations.

A famous painting of the Hanging Gardens by Charles Sheldon. Scientists have now calculated that the Babylonians could not have watered such a huge ziggurat.

ALEXANDRIA

A coin showing the Pharos of Alexandria. Coins similar to this are part of the physical evidence supporting the existence of the ancient lighthouse.

The Egyptian city of Alexandria was founded in 332 B.C. by Alexander the Great. He was too busy conquering the Middle East to spend much time in his new city. Under its Greek rulers, the Ptolemies, Alexandria became the literary and scientific center of the ancient world. Two of the world's most famous buildings were constructed there, making Alexandria a major tourist attraction. One was the great library and the other was the world's first lighthouse.

THE LIGHTHOUSE

The lighthouse was built on the island of Pharos in 280 B.C. The three-story structure, which was nearly 400 feet high, was one of the Seven Wonders of the Ancient World. The tower was built from either marble or limestone. The whole lighthouse stood on a square base. The first level was square and probably contained rooms used by the lighthouse staff. The next tier was octagonal, with a circular top level that contained the beacon fire.

Built on a square base, the lighthouse stood at least 390 feet high. The beacon light made the harbor at Alexandria one of the safest in the world.

20

This mosaic from St Mark's Cathedral, Venice, shows the saint arriving at Alexandria, guided by the light of the Pharos. The lighthouse is shown in great detail, including the front door.

A SAFE HARBOR

Inside the lighthouse was a ramp and a simple lift that carried fuel to the top of the tower. The light was provided by a beacon fire. Mirrors or metal reflectors might have been used to focus the light and direct it out to sea. The Romans copied the design and built similar lighthouses in other Mediterranean ports.

THE LIBRARY

The library was founded during the reign of Pharaoh Ptolemy I (323–283 B.C.). Ptolemy, an enthusiastic book collector, amassed about 200,000 books, mostly in the form of scrolls. His son, Ptolemy II, continued the work, sending his librarians to scour the ancient world for important works to add to the collection. A team of scholars translated foreign books into Greek. As many as 500,000 books may have been stored in the completed library.

PTOLEMY III

Ptolemy III, who reigned from 247 to 222 B.C., was even more passionate about books. All visitors to Alexandria had to hand over any manuscripts they carried. Works not already in the library were seized, and the owners given cheap copies in return. Ptolemy III even persuaded the Athenian government to lend him original manuscripts of plays by Sophocles and Euripides. He gave the Athenians a huge sum of gold as security, but then refused to return their manuscripts, sending worthless copies back to Athens.

THE MUSEUM

Ptolemy II ruled from 283 to 247 B.C. He built a great museum at Alexandria, which became an institute for research and scholarship. The Greek historian Strabo described the museum as a large complex of buildings that included lecture halls and eating rooms connected by covered walkways. The museum and library were run by priests. The scholars, who included the Greek poets Apollonius and Theocritus, and the mathematician Euclid, were paid by the government. In time, the main library was given over to the sole use of the museum scholars. Visiting scholars were forced to use a second, inferior library in the Temple of Serapis.

THE DECLINE OF ALEXANDRIA

Although Alexandria flourished under Greek rule, Egypt gradually became less important under the Romans and the city declined. The early Christians, afraid of what they called "heathen ideas" contained in the books, destroyed most of the manuscripts in the library when they burned it down in A.D. 391. The lighthouse at Alexandria was destroyed by an earthquake in 1324. The site of the lighthouse is now covered by the Islamic fort of Kait Bey, which was built in the 15th century.

The city of Alexandria had an excellent natural sheltered harbor. A small causeway to the Pharos allowed donkeys to carry fuel across for the beacon fire at the top of the lighthouse. Designed in a grid pattern, the city contained several other important buildings, such as the Temple of Serapis, the Temple of Poseidon, a mausoleum (tomb), and a theater.

SOLOMON'S TEMPLE

Three thousand years ago, the Hebrew tribes were united into a kingdom by King David. He made Jerusalem, which was a neutral city not controlled by any particular Hebrew tribe, into his capital. Around 972 B.C., David's son Solomon became king and reigned until his death in 922.

SOLOMON'S JERUSALEM

Solomon made alliances with the Egyptians and Phoenicians. Free from the threat of invasion, he transformed Jerusalem, spending some of his wealth on vast building projects such as a palace for himself and a temple. The temple was to be a permanent home for a treasure known as the Ark of the Covenant. It also became the first permanent center of the Jewish faith practiced by the Hebrews.

The Bible describes the winged guardians of the Ark as "two cherubim of olive wood, each ten cubits high...overlayed...with gold" —similar to this eighth-century B.C. carving from ancient Assyria.

The exact appearance of the Ark of the Covenant is a mystery. The stone carving (above), made nearly 1,700 years ago, shows it as an ornate chest on wheels. Illustrations of Solomon's Temple (below) have been made using details given in the Hebrew Bible. According to the First Book of Kings, "He lined the walls of the house on the inside with boards of cedar . . . and he covered the floor . . . with boards of cypress."

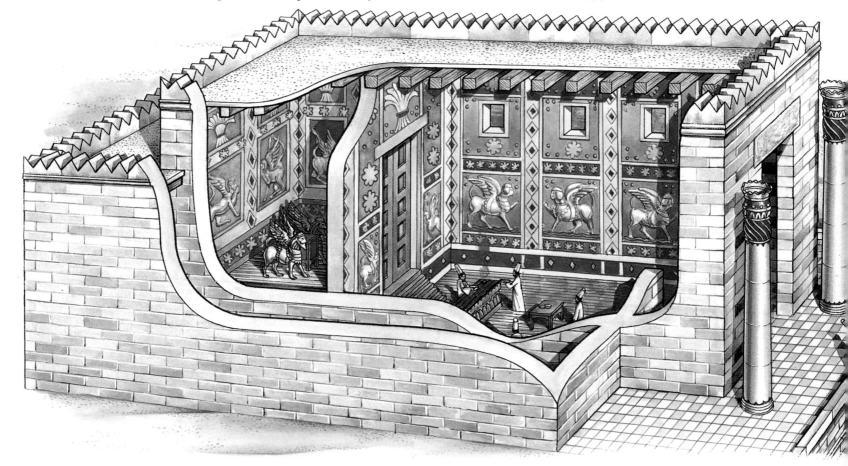

BIBLICAL REFERENCES

The temple Solomon built is described in great detail in the Hebrew Bible. From this we know the shape and size of the building, as well as many of the materials used for its construction.

The temple stood in a large courtyard near Solomon's palace. Outside the temple was a large altar for burnt offerings. Close by was a huge bronze bowl, called the "Molten Sea." Supported on the backs of twelve bronze oxen, it may have been used for ritual washing.

And the house was built of stone made ready before it was brought thither: so that there was neither hammer nor axe nor any tool of iron heard in the house, while it was in building.

— *1 Kings 6:7* —

THE TEMPLE OF SOLOMON

The temple was built of white limestone. It had a simple rectangular shape about 175 feet long, 98 feet wide, and 50 feet high. At the eastern end was a large porch. Huge bronze pillars stood on either side of the main door. Inside, the main sanctuary was lined with wood—cedar on the ceiling and cypress on the floor. Carved figures of cherubim, palm trees, and flowers decorated the walls. Tiny square windows high in the wall allowed shafts of light inside. The only furniture was a small table and an altar for burning incense.

THE HOLY OF HOLIES

At the western end of the temple was the "Holy of Holies," the most sacred place in the Hebrew world. Only the high priest was allowed through the olive-wood door into this windowless room, and then just once a year. Inside, with winged beasts on either side, stood the Ark of the Covenant.

THE ARK OF THE COVENANT

The Ark of the Covenant was a wooden chest containing the Ten Commandments inscribed on stone tablets. The ancestors of the Hebrews, who were probably nomadic herders from Mesopotamia, had carried this precious possession with them. Unlike other tribes, the Hebrews believed in just one god, Yahweh. They had worshipped their god in a tented shrine called the "tabernacle," which had also held the Ark. Solomon's temple became a permanent resting place for the Ark.

IMPORTANCE OF THE TEMPLE

Thousands of Hebrews crowded into the city throughout the year to visit the temple during the most important festivals. Solomon's temple, with its huge wooden doors overlaid with polished gold, became a symbol of the new confidence and strength of Solomon's kingdom. It was to stand for 800 years, until it was destroyed by the Romans in A.D. 70. The armies of Titus captured Jerusalem, destroyed the temple, and removed many of its treasures.

The Arch of Titus, built in the forum in Rome, is decorated with carved scenes showing the emperor's wars against the Hebrews. The armies of Titus eventually captured Jerusalem and destroyed the Temple of Solomon. Here soldiers are shown removing the large golden menorah—a seven-branched candle holder used during Hebrew festivals.

23

PETRA—CITY OF ROCK

This page shows the Roman soldier tomb in Petra. Opposite the entrance was a triclinium (a dining room where funeral feasts were held). To the left, a flight of steps curls out of the courtyard up to the garden triclinium. The illustration at top right shows the unfinished tomb façade of Ad-Dayer, "The Monastery." The inset picture below shows the inside of one of the tombs at Petra. The city is often called the "rose-red city," although the rock is also veined with other shades of red, purple, and yellow.

The ancient city of Petra lies south of the Dead Sea in what is now Jordan. Little is known about the site before about 312 B.C., when it was inhabited by the Nabataeans and prospered as a center for trade.

THE ROCK

Petra was known by many names—Requem, Selaí, and Petra. All mean "the Rock," an appropriate name, since the city was literally carved from the living rock. Because of this, much of the city remains intact, although it is no longer inhabited.

THE SUQ

Petra can only be reached through a narrow canyon called the Suq, which runs between two high mountains. The Suq was made famous in the film *Indiana Jones and the Last Crusade.* The canyon eventually opens up into a steep-sided rocky valley. The ancient inhabitants of Petra carved their houses and temples in the cliff faces.

The Roman soldier tomb
1 **Covered walkways**
2 **Triclinium**
3 **Entrance**
4 **Courtyard**
5 **Tomb**

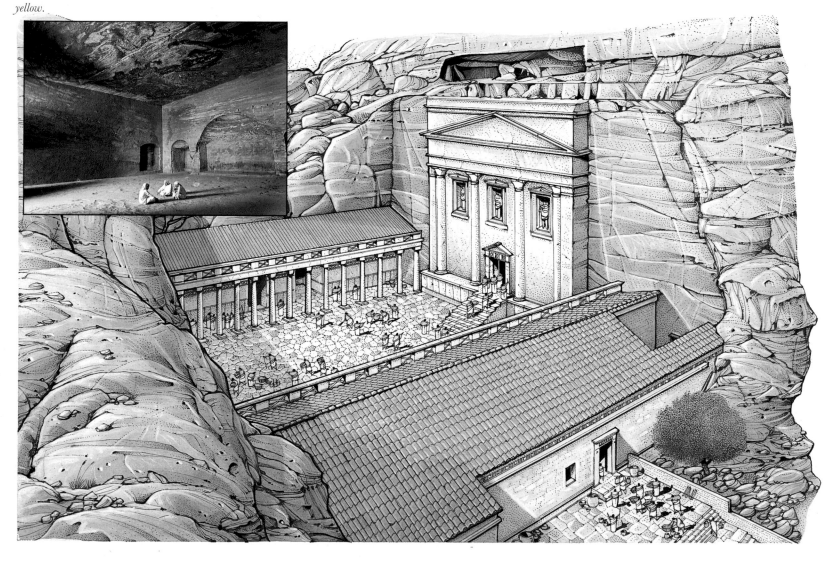

ARCHITECTURE STYLES

Many of Petra's buildings have fronts decorated with columns and statues reflecting the cultures that have had influence over the city. The architecture is a unique mixture of Persian, Assyrian, Greek, and Roman designs. Visiting architects may have designed some of the buildings. Petra also had paved streets, temples, baths, and a monumental gateway. A great market contained dozens of merchants' stalls for the traders passing through the city. Outside the buildings carved in the cliffs were many more free-standing houses built of wood and stone.

The Treasury

1 Portico
2 Inner court
3 Priests' rooms
4 The sanctuary

TRADING CITY

From about 400 B.C. to A.D. 200, Petra stood at the crossroads of two great trade caravan routes. The Nabataeans traded in Arabian perfumes, Chinese silk, and Indian spices. They were also able to tax and control all the trade passing through Petra. The city became fabulously wealthy.

PETRA IN DECLINE

In 25 B.C., the Roman emperor Augustus tried to gain control of the spice trade. By setting up a sea link between Arabia and Alexandria, he diverted land trade away from Petra and reduced the commercial importance of the city. In A.D. 363, Petra was damaged by an earthquake. It was forgotten by the outside world until about 1812, when the Swiss traveler Johann L. Burkhardt rediscovered the city.

This page shows the famous tomb façade of the Khasneh, or Treasury. The urn at the center of the façade is over nine feet wide and gave the Treasury its name. According to legend it contained treasures of gold. Travelers would even fire guns at it to release its hoard—a practice that is now forbidden by law! The inset picture below shows the Street of Façades at Petra. Although these look like little houses, the doorways are actually the entrances to tombs.

ZEUS AT OLYMPIA

Zeus was the chief of all the Greek gods. The Greeks believed he was the sender of thunder, lightning, rain, and winds. His traditional weapon was the thunderbolt, shown here.

Olympia was one of the most important sacred sites in ancient Greece. It was not only the birthplace of the Olympic Games, which, according to legend, were founded by Zeus's son Hercules, but also the home of one of the Seven Wonders of the Ancient World—a gigantic statue of Zeus.

THE HOLY SITE

Olympia became an important sacred site as early as 1600 B.C. Gradually it became the center of worship of Zeus, the king of all the Greek gods. The first Olympic games were held there in 776 B.C.

Jumping and running were the main events of the ancient Olympics. The picture on this ancient Greek storage jar shows a long jumper. The jumper did a standing jump, swinging the stone weights he held in either hand forward to give him added momentum.

The statue of Zeus was over 40 feet high. Its head nearly touched the temple ceiling. The ancient geographer and travel writer Pausanius described a spiral staircase that led to an upper floor where visitors could get a better view of the statue.

The altar of Zeus was built about 1000 B.C. on the site where, according to legend, a thunderbolt hurled by Zeus had struck the Earth. Midway through the Olympic festival, 100 oxen were sacrificed there.

THE TEMPLE OF ZEUS

The most spectacular building at Olympia was the Temple of Zeus. It was finished in about 460 B.C. and had taken about ten years to complete. The roof was supported by 34 columns. Water drained off the marble roof through waterspouts shaped like lions' heads. The building was more a shelter for a statue of Zeus than a place of worship. The inside of the temple was filled with valuables and statues offered to Zeus by kings and heroes.

THE STATUE OF ZEUS

In about 435 B.C., the Athenian sculptor Phidias began work on a colossal statue of Zeus for the temple. The statue became celebrated throughout the ancient world because of its great size and beauty. The god's skin was made of ivory plates and his robes were gold. He sat on an elaborate throne and held a sceptre with an eagle in his left hand and a statue of Nike, the goddess of victory, in his right.

In his left hand is a sceptre, skillfully wrought from a variety of metals. The sandals of the god are of gold, and so is his robe, which is decorated with animals and lilies. The throne is adorned with gold, precious stones, ebony, and ivory; it is painted and carved with figures.

—— Pausanius ——

THE OLYMPIC GAMES

The games at Olympia were held once every four years as a celebration to honor Zeus. The celebration was so important that all wars stopped and each state sent male athletes to compete. (Women were forbidden to attend.) In the first Olympics, the only athletic event was a foot race the length of the stadium, a distance of about 200 yards. Coroibus of Elis, a cook, was the first recorded winner. Gradually more events were included, such as wrestling and a pentathlon consisting of running, jumping, spear throwing, discus throwing, and wrestling. Later, boxing, chariot racing, and horse racing were added. By 632 B.C., the games had expanded to five days of competition.

THE END OF THE GAMES

Gradually the simple aims of the original games were lost. Winners became national heroes who had statues of themselves erected. In A.D. 394, the games were officially ended by the Roman emperor Theodosius, who felt that they were un-Christian. The temple of Zeus was destroyed in A.D. 426 and the statue was destroyed by fire in A.D. 462. Olympia and the Olympic ideals were not rediscovered for over 1,000 years.

One of the toughest races in the ancient Olympics was run in full armor. For most other races athletes competed naked. This was to glorify the human body and to make sure that all the athletes were men. Women could compete in their own version of the Olympics, the Games of Hera.

Chariot racing took place in the Olympic stadium. Built in the fourth century B.C., it seated 40,000 spectators on sloping grassy banks.

HARBOR AT CARTHAGE

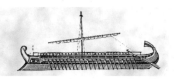

An ancient glass charm from Carthage. The Phoenicians' name came from their most precious cargo—purple dye made from the Murex sea snail. The Greeks called these people "Phoinikes," which means "Purple Men."

The harbor at Carthage (right) as it was in its prime. The outer rectangular harbor housed cargo ships; the inner, circular harbor was designed for warships.

The city of Carthage in North Africa was a colony set up by the Phoenicians. They were a seafaring race who originally came from the land of Canaan, now modern Lebanon. Carthage began as a trading port but developed into the greatest power in the western Mediterranean to challenge the might of Rome. The foundation of Carthaginian power was its large navy and the best organized naval base in the ancient world.

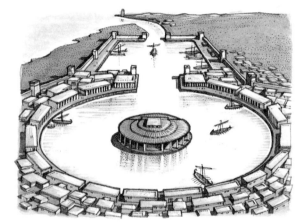

THE PHOENICIANS

Having little fertile land of their own, the Phoenicians took to the sea and became superb traders. From as early as 2950 B.C., their galleys sailed around the coast of the Mediterranean carrying dried fish, gold, ivory, glass, cloth, jewelry, and metal goods.

CARTHAGE

The city of Carthage was founded by the Phoenicians around 814 B.C. The name means "new city" in Phoenician. It was surrounded by walls over 20 miles long. There was an inner citadel on a hill known as Byrsa. About 700,000 people lived at Carthage, although many of them probably lived outside the main city walls. The wonder at Carthage was its magnificent artificial harbor, known as the "cothon."

Some reconstructions of the cothon show a jetty running from the inner circular harbor to the shore. Without a jetty, warships would have sent most of the crew ashore in rowboats. A skeleton crew would then row the ship to the central harbor.

THE COTHON

At this time, most harbors were in natural bays and consisted of simple jetties with a few warehouses for storage. The harbor at Carthage was by far the largest manmade harbor in the ancient world. It consisted of two huge lagoons that were dug out by the Carthaginians. The larger outer lagoon contained a rectangular harbor for merchant ships. The inner circular lagoon was designed for warships called quinqueremes (page 28 top right), which were rowed by over 200 oarsmen.

THE SHIPYARD

The round harbor was the largest naval base in the ancient world. In the center of the lagoon was a circular island built of stone. This contained roofed slipways that could hold the warships under cover.

Once a ship had been drawn up on a slipway, it was almost invisible from the town, and could be easily cleaned and repaired away from any spies watching the Carthaginian army. On top of the slipways was a large admiralty building. From here lookouts watched the ships in the harbor and controlled the traffic with trumpets and shouting, and with torches at night.

GREATNESS AND DECLINE

In 264 B.C., the city began the first of three wars with its great rival, Rome, called the Punic (Phoenician) Wars. By the end of the third Punic War in 146 B.C., Carthage had been left a smoking ruin. Its fields were sown with salt to sterilize the earth so the city could not become powerful again.

However, under the Roman Empire, Carthage became very wealthy and contained even more people than before. In A.D. 533, Carthage was captured by Belisarius, a Byzantine general. It remained a Christian Byzantine stronghold until A.D. 698, when it was destroyed by Muslim conquerors.

Phoenician traders brought cedar wood to Egypt as early as 2950 B.C. The Bible (Kings 1 5:8) mentions that Phoenician galleys even carried the cedar logs used to build the Temple of Solomon.

THE SEVEN WONDERS

The Parthenon was the temple dedicated to Athena, the goddess of Athens. It was not included on the original list of Seven Wonders. However it is now considered to be one of the most glorious buildings of the ancient world.

The original Seven Wonders of the World were the seven greatest feats of ancient technology, architecture, and art as they were recorded by Greek and Roman authors.

PHILO'S LIST

The original list of wonders appeared about 130 B.C. in a poem by Antipater of Sidon. The wonders were listed as the Pyramids of Egypt, the Walls and the Hanging Gardens of Babylon, the Temple of Artemis at Ephesus, the Statue of Zeus at Olympia, the Mausoleum at Halicarnassus, and the Colossus of Rhodes. A mathematician, Philo of Byzantium, listed the Pharos of Alexandria instead of the Walls of Babylon. Philo's list is often considered the most important. Other writers copied this list, combining the Walls and Hanging Gardens into one wonder.

OTHER WONDERS

Other marvels included the Altar of the Sun God at Pergamum, the Stadium at Olympia, the Parthenon at Athens, the Theater at Epidaurus, and the four-mile-long slipway across the Isthmus of Corinth along which the Greeks hauled their ships to avoid a 400-mile-long voyage.

The Temple of Artemis was decorated with magnificent works of art showing characters from Greek myths. Tall, slim columns supported the tiled roof.

We know roughly what the Mausoleum at Halicarnassus looked like from ancient writings and the recreations done by modern archaeologists. The tomb was designed by Greek architects and decorated with Greek sculptures and carvings.

The Temple of Artemis is the only house of the gods. Whoever looks will be convinced that the heavenly world of immortality has been placed on the earth.

— *Philo* —

TEMPLE OF ARTEMIS

The Temple of Artemis was built at Ephesus (now in modern Turkey) about 550 B.C. by Croesus, the King of Lydia. The inner part of the temple housed a simple statue of the goddess Artemis made of black stone decorated with gold and silver. The temple was destroyed by fire in 356 B.C. by a madman named Herostratus. It was then rebuilt, and was destroyed again by invading Goths in A.D. 262. Its remains were discovered in 1866.

THE MAUSOLEUM

There are few remains of another ancient wonder, the Mausoleum at Halicarnassus, in modern Turkey. It was built by Queen Artemesia around 350 B.C. to honor her dead husband, Mausolus. The tomb made such an impression on the world that the word "mausoleum" is still used today to describe a large tomb. The tomb looked like a tall, square temple standing on a square base. It was decorated with columns and statues. The roof was a 24-step pyramid crowned by the statue of a chariot and horses, which towered 160 feet above the town. The Mausoleum was destroyed by an earthquake in the 13th century.

THE COLOSSUS OF RHODES

In 305 B.C., the citizens of the island of Rhodes built a huge statue to celebrate their survival after a siege by the Macedonians. This "Colossus" stood over 100 feet tall. It represented the sun god, Helios, and probably wore a crown shaped like the sun's rays. Cast in bronze, the statue is often shown in pictures straddling the mouth of the harbor at Rhodes. It is unlikely that ancient builders could have made a statue large enough to do this, and historians now think that the Colossus probably stood on a dock beside the harbor. Although reinforced with stone and iron, the Colossus broke at the knees

Sixty-six years after its erection, the statue fell over in an earthquake, but even lying down it is a marvel. Few people can get their arms around one of its thumbs, and its fingers are bigger than most statues.

Pliny the Younger

Greek theaters were wonderful buildings. One of the best surviving examples is the theater at Epidaurus. Built after 350 B.C., it could hold 14,000 spectators on the giant horseshoe-shaped terraces.

and fell in an earthquake about 66 years after it was finished. The citizens were warned by an oracle not to rebuild it. When Arabs invaded Rhodes in A.D. 672, the Colossus was broken up and sold for scrap metal—a sad end for one of the original Seven Wonders of the World!

The Colossus of Rhodes was probably a hollow statue. The main structure could have been a wooden frame covered with bronze plates to form the shape of the Colossus.

31

ROMAN WONDERS

The Emperor Vespasian ordered the building of the Colosseum in Rome as an arena for gladiatorial games. To protect the spectators from the heat of the sun, the arena could be covered by a canvas awning that was pulled into place by 1,000 sailors using ropes and pulleys.

The Romans were skillful, efficient builders who also adapted ideas from other people. Various emperors transformed the city of Rome itself into a wonder of the ancient world.

THE CITY OF ROME

The Romans called Rome "Urbs," which is Latin for "the city." At its height, Rome was a teeming metropolis of over a million people, with palaces, stadiums, temples, and shopping malls. Great public buildings were usually built by order of the emperor. Many of the roads, fortifications, and public buildings outside Rome were built by the army, partly to keep the soldiers fit and occupied, and partly to improve the defenses of the empire. Everything was built to last, using brick, stone, and concrete.

THE COLOSSEUM

Roman emperors kept the restless population of Rome under control with free monthly handouts of grain and plenty of entertainment, such as plays, athletic contests, games, and circuses. The arena for gladiatorial games was the Colosseum.

It took about ten years to build the arena, which was finished in A.D. 80. The Colosseum held up to 55,000 spectators. It was made mainly of stone and huge amounts of concrete. Some parts, such as the seats for the senators, were surfaced with marble. The top gallery, which was for women only, was built of wood. Under the arena was a maze of rooms and cages for wild animals. The animals could be brought to the surface using lifts.

The Circus Maximus was the chief chariot-racing stadium in Rome. The stadium had stone terraces, but sometimes wooden seating may have been added to make extra rows. In one accident, these seats collapsed, killing 13,000 people.

THE CIRCUS MAXIMUS

People could also watch chariot racing in the Circus Maximus, or "Great Circus," which was the chariot-racing arena in ancient Rome. It was a giant U-shaped track with a wall down the center, surrounded by banked seats on three sides. The arena was rebuilt several times. It reached its greatest size during the reign of the Emperor Constantine in the fourth century A.D. when it was about 2,260 feet long by 620 feet wide. It held nearly 250,000 spectators, making it one of the largest arenas ever built.

NERO'S PALACE

The Emperor Nero's "Golden House" was one of the most luxurious Roman palaces. Built in the heart of Rome on the most expensive land, the hallway was so tall that it easily held a statue of Nero that was 120 feet high. The dining rooms' ceilings were made of ivory panels that could open to shower the guests with perfumed flowers. The main banquet hall revolved night and day —probably driven by water.

In the Roman Empire, most villas, forts, and towns had their own mills for grinding corn. There were at least 20 in Rome. The largest watermill was at Barbegal, in southern France (above). It had 16 waterwheels that turned eight millstones, grinding enough grain to feed 12,500 people each day.

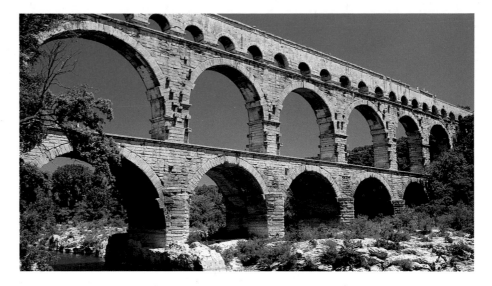

One of the largest aqueducts of the Roman Empire was the three-story Pont du Gard in France. The channel carried by the aqueduct was 30 miles long and flowed into a reservoir that could hold 22,000 tons of water.

THE PANTHEON

This "Temple of All the Gods" was built by Hadrian about A.D. 120, and was constructed almost entirely of concrete. It was a circular building with a shallow domed roof made of overlapping concrete rings. Surprisingly, the center of the dome was open. This made the roof lighter and prevented it from crashing down on visitors.

BATHS OF CARACALLA

The Romans conducted business at the bathhouses. The largest and most beautiful baths in Rome were finished during the reign of Emperor Caracalla in A.D. 216. The building could contain more than 1,500 bathers at once, with amenities ranging from steam rooms to cold water plunges.

TRAJAN'S COLUMN

Trajan's Column is 100 feet high and made from 20 enormous blocks of marble, fitted one on top of the other. The façade is decorated with more than 2,500 carved figures that depict the Emperor Trajan's wars in Dacia. The base of the column is shaped like a hollow cube and contains several rooms, along with a winding staircase that leads to the top.

Trajan's Column as it looks today. It is covered with carved scenes (see bas-relief page 32 top right), and has a spiral staircase that leads to the top (inset).

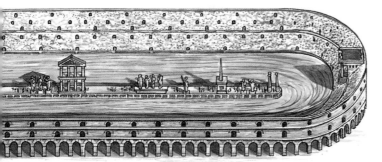

AMERICAN WONDERS

Scientists have built a working hot-air balloon out of materials available to the Nazca people at the time they made their strange lines. Perhaps the Nazca designers hovered high above the desert, shouting instructions to workers below.

The first humans probably came to North America about **50,000** years ago. They walked from Asia to the Americas across a land bridge that connected the two continents at the time. It took their descendants many thousands of years to spread into every corner of North and South America, where they created many amazing sites.

THE NAZCA LINES

On the arid edge of the Atacama desert, the Nazca tribe (200 B.C.–A.D. 600) created the shapes of gigantic creatures and geometric forms on the ground. No one knows why or how they made these shapes. The patterns are almost invisible on the ground and can only be seen in their entirety from the air. Some scientists have speculated that the lines were drawn as messages to the gods.

The Nazca lines were scratched in the desert surface. They have been preserved by the extreme dryness of the region. Many show geometric shapes and huge animals, including a monkey, a bird, and a spider (above). The lines are hundreds of feet long, and can only be seen in their entirety from the air.

THE FIRST PEOPLE TO FLY?

Scientists have even suggested that the Nazca might have built hot-air balloons so that observers could fly high above the plain and instruct the workers far below. There is slight evidence to support this idea, but if it is true, the South Americans may have been the first people to fly!

HOPEWELL CULTURE

In North America, many tribes built gigantic burial mounds. The tribes are known collectively as the Hopewell (200 B.C.–A.D. 500) after the first mound that was investigated. Many mounds were simple burial places, each one containing a single ancestor. Some bodies were buried in log tombs that were later set on fire, or they were cremated in clay ovens before being covered with earth mounds. The bodies were usually buried with personal possessions, such as pottery and jewelery.

MOUND BUILDERS

The shape and size of the mounds varies. One group at Mound City, Ohio, contains dozens of mounds enclosed by a rectangular earth wall. Some of these mounds had simple geometric forms, or may even have been earthworks or forts. Other mounds were much larger pyramid shapes, thought to have been the bases for wooden temples or other religious buildings. Perhaps the most intriguing mounds are those built in the shapes of animals. These more elaborate mounds, such as the Great Serpent Mound in Ohio, were probably important religious centers or possibly feasting grounds.

PYRAMIDS OF THE SUN

In Central America, various tribes such as the Maya, the Olmecs, and the Toltecs built stone cities. The largest was at Teotihuacán in Mexico, where the people worshipped cruel, elemental gods—such as the rain god and the sun god. They built gigantic stone pyramid temples on which to hold their ceremonies.

These great buildings rising from the water, all made of stone, seemed like an enchanted vision. It was all so wonderful . . . this first glimpse of things never heard of, seen, or dreamed of before.

Bernal Diaz

TENOCHTITLÁN

At Tenochtitlán, the Aztecs built a floating city. A ceremonial center of stone buildings was founded on islands in Lake Texcoco. Here was the great temple where thousands of victims were sacrificed each year, their hearts torn out as offerings to the sun god. Surrounding the city was a fertile plain of gardens and fields that literally floated on rafts anchored to each other. Sewage was collected as fertilizer for these fields, and fresh water was piped into the city. The Spanish conquerors, led by Hernan Cortés, were amazed by the beauty of the city when they first saw it in 1519. The quotation above was written by one of these Spanish soldiers, Bernal Diaz.

The Great Serpent Mound in Ohio is probably the most complicated Hopewell Mound. It is shaped like a giant serpent swallowing an egg. The snake, which is wriggling northward, is over 1,300 feet long and six feet high.

ROADS AND TERRACES

In Peru, the Incas ruled a sprawling empire. They built giant stone terraces so they could grow food in mountainous areas. They constructed huge reservoirs and a network of canals to irrigate dry lands. They built magnificent cities out of stones cut so precisely that a knife blade could not be driven into the cracks between them.

The Incas also constructed a network of paved roads even longer than those built by the Romans. Dizzying suspension bridges spanned gigantic ravines. A stream of water ran at the side of each road to refresh weary travelers. Messengers ran between relay stations, carrying news up and down a road over 3,200 miles long, which ran the entire length of the Inca Empire.

Native Americans used elaborate pipes for ceremonial smoking. The soapstone pipe on the left is from Oklahoma, and is carved in the shape of a warrior beheading a victim. The pipe on the far left is in the shape of a toad. It is typical of the pipes carved by the Hopewell Indians, who often decorated pipes and pottery with images of birds, fish, and other animals. They also made beautiful objects out of copper and gold, such as the pearl-eyed raven on page 34 top right.

EASTER ISLAND STATUES

The statues had eyes made of white coral with pupils of red volcanic rock. The eyes were the last things to be added to the statue when it was put up, perhaps to "bring it to life."

Some time later, a second group arrived, probably from South America, about 2,500 miles away. In 1947, Norwegian explorer Thor Heyerdahl made the long voyage from South America in a balsa wood raft to prove that South Americans could have reached the island. The presence of sweet potatoes, which are found in the Americas but could not have drifted to the island, seems to back up Heyerdahl's theory.

LONG EARS AND SHORT EARS

According to the islanders' own legends, they somehow became divided into two groups—the Long Ears and the Short Ears. This seems to support the idea that there were originally two different groups of inhabitants.

These early inhabitants lived by fishing and farming. They were able to work and shape stone with great skill, and built stone terraces that faced the sun, suggesting that they may have been sun worshippers. They also built stone houses that were circular, oval, or boat-shaped.

Some of the statues on Easter Island weigh up to 50 tons and would have been moved several miles from the quarries where they were carved. One way the islanders might have moved the statues was by pulling on ropes to make the statues rock and twist so that they appeared to "walk" along. The topknots, made of red volcanic rock, may have been tied in place before the statues were put up, since it would have been hard to lift them separately.

Easter Island is one of the loneliest and most mysterious places in the world. What brought people to this remote Pacific island is a puzzle. But even stranger is the story of the gigantic stone heads that stare silently across the empty land.

THE FIRST INHABITANTS

The first people to come to Easter Island arrived around A.D. 400. They were Polynesian sailors who must have made an epic voyage across thousands of miles of open ocean.

THE STATUES

In about A.D. 1100, the islanders began to build giant stone statues. The statues had long heads and long ears and were placed facing inland all around the island on ceremonial platforms called "ahus." Each statue had a red topknot or headdress that was added separately and huge eyes made of white coral. The statues were carved from volcanic rock using simple stone tools.

MOVING THE STATUES

The rock came from quarries inside the volcano of Rano Raraku. For many years, scientists puzzled over how the islanders could have moved the huge stones. Thor Heyerdahl asked the islanders, who showed him how a few people using ropes could "walk" the statues along in an upright position by rocking them from side to side while pulling them forward.

CIVIL WAR AND FAMINE

While making the statues, the islanders started to cut down the island's trees. Perhaps this was to clear land for farming or to make roofs for the houses or levers to move the giant statues. Unfortunately, it was an environmental disaster that had a terrible effect on the land. Without tree roots to hold it together, the soil began to wash away. Around 1680, there was a major famine followed by a terrible war between the Long Ears and the Short Ears. Statue-building stopped and many of the statues were toppled over. Islanders took refuge in underground hideaways, and some may have become cannibals. The population on the island began to decline. By the time the first Europeans arrived at Easter Island in 1722, there were only a few people, some simple huts, and toppled statues left.

A line of statues on Easter Island. When Captain Cook visited the island in the 18th century, the islanders told him that each statue had a name. Ancestor worship is common in the Pacific, and it seems likely that it was practiced on Easter Island.

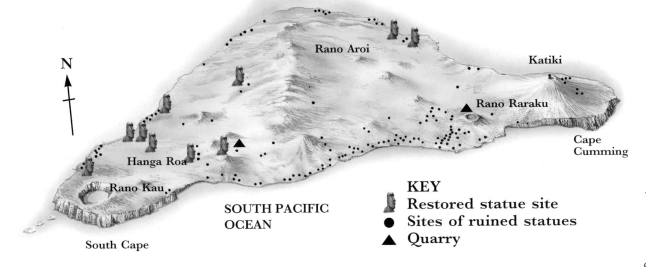

Rano Aroi

Katiki

Rano Raraku

Cape Cumming

Hanga Roa

Rano Kau

SOUTH PACIFIC OCEAN

South Cape

KEY
🗿 **Restored statue site**
● **Sites of ruined statues**
▲ **Quarry**

This map shows the sites of the statues and the quarries on the island. There are remains of about 600 statues on Easter Island, mostly between 10 and 20 feet high. The largest is 36 feet high. About 150 statues were never finished and remain half-carved in the quarries.

CHICHÉN ITZÁ

This Toltec wall painting shows a warrior and the feathered serpent god, Quetzalcoatl. The Great Pyramid at Chichén Itzá was dedicated to this god.

In a remote part of the Yucatán peninsula in Mexico, the city of Chichén Itzá was once a spectacular ceremonial center for the Maya and Toltec Indians. A thousand years ago, Toltecs watched as human sacrifices were hurled into the sacred well as offerings to the rain god, Chac.

THE CITY
Chichén Itzá, which is now in ruins, is located in northeastern Mexico. Founded about A.D. 432 by the Maya, the city was built on a flat plain on a site chosen because it contained two enormous natural wells. The name of the city, which means "Mouths of the Wells of the Itzá," comes from the Mayan words "chi," meaning "mouth," "chén," meaning "wells," and "Itzá," one of the many tribes that lived there.

The city center of Chichén Itzá showing the Great Pyramid Temple of Quetzalcoatl (center left), the "Snail" tower (center), and the sacred ball court (left).

THE MAYA
The first inhabitants, the Maya, built many large ceremonial buildings at Chichén Itzá, including palaces, sweat baths, and pyramid temples dedicated to the serpent and jaguar gods. Maya priests regularly made human sacrifices on altars on the tops of these temple pyramids, cutting out their victims' hearts as offerings to the sun.

They also built a very unusual round tower known as the "Snail" because of the spiral staircase that wound around inside it. The building, which stands 400 feet high, may have been used as an observatory to study the night sky. The rulers, military leaders, and priests lived in the city—ordinary people lived outside it.

THE TOLTECS

Around 950, the city was taken over by a tribe called the Toltecs. They were accompanied or followed later by the Itzá. These people constructed many wonderful new buildings, including a gigantic sacred ball court, the Great Pyramid Temple dedicated to the feathered serpent god Quetzalcoatl, and the Temple of the Warriors with its doorway guarded by giant open-mouthed feathered serpents. A carved reclining figure of Chac, the rain god (see page 38 top right), lies outside the temple, holding its offering bowl up to the skies.

THE BALL COURT

The ball court at Chichén Itzá was the largest in Central America. It is 420 feet long and about 200 feet wide. Surrounded by a high wall, the sacred games held there were probably watched only by nobles standing on wooden viewing platforms.

THE WELLS

Chichén Itzá had two giant wells or "cenotes." One well was used to supply water to the city, but the other had a

A ceremonial ballgame. Playing with a rubber ball, the players tried to score goals by putting the ball through a stone hoop high on one wall. Carvings on the wall suggest that the losing team was probably executed as a sacrifice to the serpent god.

darker purpose. During the Toltec period, people made sacrifices to the rain god. Offerings of jade and gold were thrown into the well, but there were also stories of human sacrifices.

VANISHING PEOPLE

When the Toltecs came to the city, they found it abandoned by the Maya who had built it. No one knows where the original inhabitants went. Around 1224, the Toltecs themselves abandoned the city. There are no signs of violence and no evidence of an attack. The people seem to have simply vanished into thin air.

One of the great cenotes. Archaeologists investigating the city have discovered over 40 human skeletons, probably human sacrifices, at the bottom of one of the wells.

The Great Pyramid Temple had a secret passage leading to a hidden room. A lifesized statue of the red jaguar god, with spots made of disks of polished jade, was found inside.

39

HAGIA SOPHIA

After Rome was captured by the Germanic Visigoths in A.D. 410, the center of the Christian world shifted to the Byzantine Empire. In 532, its emperor, Justinian, ordered the building of a great church in the capital city of Constantinople. Called Hagia Sophia, which meant "Holy Wisdom" in Greek, this magnificent building was to be a rallying point for Christianity. For nearly 1,000 years, it was the most important church of the Byzantine Empire.

THE SITE

A church had stood on the site chosen for Hagia Sophia since A.D. 360. But in 532, two opposing groups of chariot racing fans began to quarrel. The arguments soon got out of hand and grew into a major riot. By the time Justinian had restored order, many important buildings, including the original Hagia Sophia, had been destroyed.

THE ARCHITECTS

Justinian commissioned two architects, Anthemius of Tralles and Isidorous of Miletos, to design and build a new church. These two men were master builders and experts in geometry and mechanics. Their design was revolutionary. They decided to make the interior of the church one huge open space. Instead of having a long building with the roof supported on lines of pillars, they designed the roof as a series of domes. The main dome was 100 feet wide and over 200 feet high!

The illustration at the top of the page shows the emperor Justinian (center) with Archbishop Maximilian (left) and a deacon (right). The emperor, important church officials, and hundreds of ordinary worshippers attended religious services at Hagia Sophia. The emperor led the procession into the church and listened to sermons spoken from the round pulpit.

THE DOMES

Drawing on Roman methods for building domes from concrete, the architects created a huge shallow central dome supported by half domes that acted as buttresses. The domes were surrounded on all sides by an outer shell of aisles and galleries that allowed the roof to arch out to create a vast open interior space. Bays containing high windows allowed light to flood in at any time of the day or year.

THE CHURCH COMPLETED

The church took only five years to build, and visitors were astounded by it. They described the church as "seemingly suspended as if by a golden chain from heaven." Hagia Sophia became a magnificent stage for the elaborate processions of Byzantine church services.

THE FALL OF THE CITY

In 557, an earthquake destroyed part of the dome. Isidorous was still alive and able to supervise the repairs. In 1453, Constantinople was captured by the Ottoman Turks. They added tall thin towers called minarets to the outside of the church, and altered the interior to create a magnificent Islamic mosque.

The exterior of Hagia Sophia as it can be seen today, showing the minarets added by the Ottoman Turks.

1	West entrance	6	Half dome
2	Round pulpit	7	Main dome
3	Sanctuary	8	Drum supporting
4	Galleries		main dome
5	Aisle	9	High windows

BOROBUDUR

The Buddha was a prince who gave up his wealth after witnessing death, famine, old age, and disease for the first time. Through meditation he found enlightenment and spent the rest of his life spreading his teachings, which form the ideas behind the Buddhist religion.

The huge Buddhist shrine of Borobudur rises from the surrounding jungle of central Java like a staircase leading to heaven. This wondrous shrine, shaped something like a stepped pyramid, is a complicated symbol of the life of the Buddha.

THE BUDDHA
The Buddha was an Indian prince who lived about 2,500 years ago. He taught his followers that they must live many lives on earth until they become good enough to reach a state of perfect peace and spiritual freedom called "nirvana." Borobudur is a symbol of this idea.

THE HOLY HILL
In about A.D. 800, Borobudur was built in Java, in Asia, by a king of the powerful and wealthy Sailendra dynasty. The great shrine is built from dark gray volcanic stone. It sits on, and entirely covers, a small hill. The base of the monument is 160,000 square feet. On it rests a series of giant steps or tiers. Each tier is a terrace connected by four stairways to the tiers above and below.

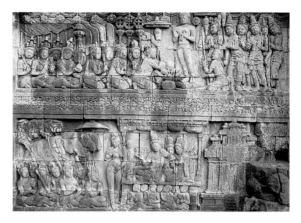

Around each terrace, the walls are covered with ornate carvings. They show moral lessons, episodes from the Buddha's life, and, on the higher terraces, spiritual scenes.

THE SHAPE OF BOROBUDUR
The shrine is based on the mandala, a mystic Buddhist symbol of the universe which combines the square as earth and the circle as heaven. The plan of Borobudur is therefore a circle within a square, which can clearly be seen when the shrine is viewed from the air (see below). Around each terrace runs a roofless corridor, the walls of which are lined with ornate carvings. These carvings show the Buddha's development and struggle to reach perfection.

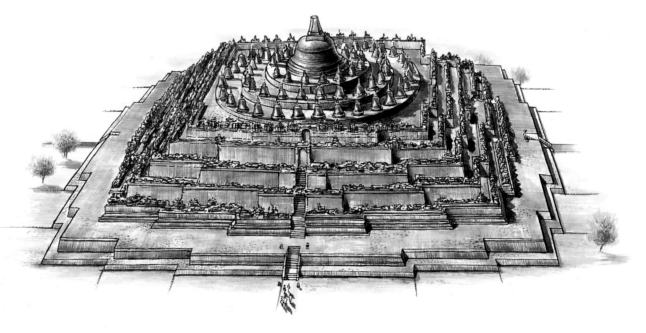

Borobudur from the air. It was built with over 500,000 cubic feet of gray volcanic stone and was over 100 feet high. Borobudur was abandoned after A.D. 1000. A massive restoration project was started in 1975, when it was discovered that water seepage threatened to damage the site.

PILGRIMAGES

When pilgrims visit Borobudur, they walk around the monument in a clockwise direction, completely circling each terrace before climbing to the next. As the pilgrims walk around, they pass the carvings. By examining them they learn the story of the Buddha's life, as well as lessons on how to reach perfection in their own lives. By doing this, each pilgrim "lives" one life and then climbs to the next. The slow climb toward the top of Borobudur represents the efforts believers must make to improve themselves and move gradually upward toward nirvana.

NIRVANA

The upper three terraces are circular. They do not have walled corridors, but instead are open and spacious. These terraces represent the stage of spiritual enlightenment, or nirvana, that Buddhists are striving to reach.

STUPAS

On the terraces there are 72 stupas. Usually, stupas are solid bell-shaped domes that contain relics of the Buddha or other saints. But many of the stupas at Borobudur are domes made of pierced stone latticework. Inside each of these domes, just visible through the holes, sits a meditating stone Buddha. A giant solid stupa sits in the center of the topmost terrace, crowning the monument. This represents the pinnacle of Buddhist enlightenment.

The final tier at Borobudur is 100 feet high. Here, within latticework stupas, sit statues of the Buddha similar to this one, and to the one in the cutaway on page 42 top right.

Pilgrims at Borobudur. Each pilgrim makes nine clockwise circuits around the monument because this number is mystical to Buddhists.

WONDERS AT NARA

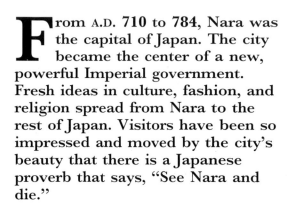

From A.D. **710** to **784,** Nara was the capital of Japan. The city became the center of a new, powerful Imperial government. Fresh ideas in culture, fashion, and religion spread from Nara to the rest of Japan. Visitors have been so impressed and moved by the city's beauty that there is a Japanese proverb that says, "See Nara and die."

IMPERIAL CAPITAL

Before A.D. 600, Japanese noble families held much of the country's power. But in 645, Prince Naka-no-Oe became emperor and began to consolidate power. His adviser introduced great changes. For the first time, instead of each new monarch having a new capital city, there would be a permanent Imperial city. Nara was chosen as this site.

The seated Buddha inside the Daibutsuden Hall at the Todai-ji Temple at Nara. The present statue was made in 1708 as a smaller replacement for the original, which was destroyed by fire.

Like many old Japanese buildings, the temples and monasteries at Nara were made of wood. These wooden buildings were so light that they were less likely to be destroyed by earthquakes. However, they were a fire hazard. This scene shows the monks at the Todai-ji Temple trying to save the buildings as they are consumed by fire after being struck by lightning.

44

THE CITY OF NARA

The city was built to be perfect right from the start, and designed to show the order and power of the emperor's rule. It was laid out as a grid containing palaces, government offices, storehouses, granaries, markets, temples, and pagodas (see page 44 top right). The buildings were magnificent, with overhanging roofs and ornately carved decorations. They also reflected Chinese ideas and fashions that had become popular in Japan at this time.

THE TODAI-JI

The most magnificent temple at Nara was the Todai-ji. Inside was the Daibutsuden, or Great Buddha Hall. Originally the Buddha Hall was painted red. It contained the Daibutsu, a huge seated Buddha that was over 50 feet high. Cast in bronze, the statue weighed 605 tons. The halo surrounding the statue contained the images of 1,000 Buddhas.

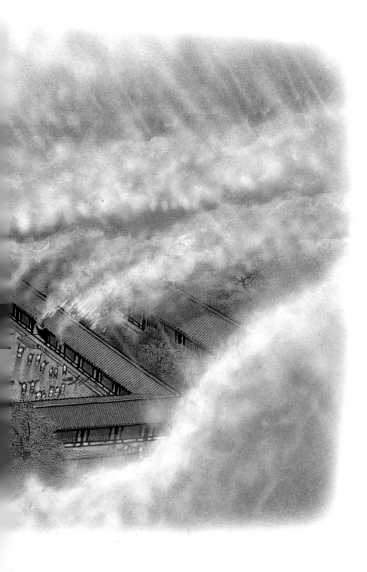

CENTER OF LEARNING

Seven great Buddhist temples and other lesser ones were built at Nara. As well as being spiritual buildings, they were also great centers of learning. Chinese medicine, astrology, and technology were taught and studied. Scholars adapted Chinese characters to provide the first system for writing down the spoken Japanese language. Monks from Nara traveled all over Japan, spreading these new ideas.

THE TOSHODAIJI

The most famous monk at Nara was the Chinese Chien Chen. In 742 he was invited by the emperor to visit Japan and instruct the priests. His teachings revolutionized Japan. The emperor ordered a monastery, the Toshodaiji, to be built as a center for his teaching.

BEAUTIFUL CITY

In 784, the capital was transferred to nearby Kyoto because the monks had become too powerful and interfered with the government of the country. But Nara remained an important spiritual center.

It took Chien Chen 11 years to leave China, and on his travels he suffered betrayal, shipwreck, and blindness. The Toshodaiji monastery was built as a center for his teachings. The buildings were painted red, green, blue, and gold (above). At Nara, scholars adapted Chinese characters to the Japanese language. The eighth-century map below shows a combination of Chinese and Japanese characters.

KEY DATES AND GLOSSARY

T he wonders of the ancient world were visited by tourists just as sites of interest are today. Over time many have been destroyed by natural disaster or invading armies. Many of the dates given here are approximate because precise records do not exist.

The three pyramids at Giza: from left to right, pyramid of Menkaure, pyramid of Khephren, and the Great Pyramid of Cheops (see also pages 8–11). The Sphinx appears beside the three tombs built for the wives of Cheops. In the foreground, the Egyptians irrigate their land using water from the sacred river of the Nile.

B.C.
c8000 City and walls of Jericho built.
c5000 Earliest ziggurat built at Eridu.
c3300 Stonehenge used as a ceremonial or religious center.
c3000 Work begun on megalithic monument at Carnac; first settlers at Troy.
c2550 Work begun on the Great Pyramid at Giza for the Pharaoh Cheops.
c2100 Ziggurat built at Ur.
c2010 Mentuhotpe I buried at Deir el Bahri.
c1700 Palace at Knossos built.
1450 Volcano on Thera erupted and palace at Knossos buried under ash.
c950 Temple built by Solomon in Jerusalem.
814 Phoenicians founded city of Carthage.
776 First official Olympic games held.
605–562 Nebuchadnezzar II ruled Babylon and built the Hanging Gardens.

c550 Temple of Artemis built.
c435 Phidias started making the statue of Zeus for the Temple in Olympia.
c350 Mausoleum built at Halicarnassus.
332 Alexandria founded by Alexander the Great.
312 Nabataeans first inhabited Petra.
305 Colossus of Rhodes built.
280 Lighthouse at Alexandria built.
c200 First Hopewell mounds built; Nazca lines made.
130 Original list of the Seven Wonders of the World appeared in poem by Antipater.
A.D.
70 Solomon's Temple destroyed by the Romans.
80 Colosseum in Rome completed.
363 Petra damaged by an earthquake.
c400 The last city of Troy fell in ruins; first inhabitants arrived at Easter Island.
426 Temple of Zeus at Olympia destroyed.
432 Mayas founded city of Chichén Itzá.
462 Statue of Zeus destroyed by fire.
532 Emperor Justinian ordered building of Hagia Sophia in Constantinople.
672 Arabs invaded Rhodes, and Colossus broken up for scrap metal.
c698 Harbor at Carthage destroyed by Muslim conquerors.

710 Nara became capital of Japan; Todai-ji temple and Toshodaiji monastery built.

c800 Borobudur built in Asia.

1224 Toltecs abandoned Chichén Itzá.

1324 Lighthouse at Alexandria destroyed by an earthquake.

1453 Constantinople captured by the Turks and Hagia Sophia made an Islamic mosque.

1722 First Europeans arrived at Easter Island to find only a few inhabitants.

Glossary

Beaker Culture: a group of people who lived in Europe c3000 B.C., named after the distinctive pottery beakers they made.

bas-relief: a scene that stands out slightly from the flat surface on which it is carved.

bitumen: a naturally occurring tar used for waterproofing.

Bronze Age: a time at the end of the Stone Age when bronze first came into regular use. In Europe the Bronze Age began about 1800 B.C.

buttress: a support or prop.

colossus: from the Greek "kolossus," meaning "giant statue."

isthmus: a narrow strip of land that connects two pieces of land together.

latticework: a crisscross section with diamond-shaped hole in it.

meditation: deep thought.

megalith: monument made of giant stones.

minarets: a tall tower connected to a mosque, from which people are called to prayer.

mosque: a Moslem temple.

oracle: a person, priest, or shrine through which a god is supposed to speak.

pilgrim: someone who visits holy places.

scribe: a writer.

solstice: the times of the year when the sun is nearest to or farthest from the equator.

Stone Age: a time when people made and used stone tools and weapons. The Stone Age began over one million years ago.

sweat baths: steam-filled rooms where the heat opens the pores of the skin and causes dirt to be sweated off the body.

talent: a unit of money used in the ancient world.

Quotations

The Greek historian Herodotus wrote the quotation on page 10. The speech about Troy (page 14) comes from a translation of the *Iliad* by Homer. Pausanius (page 27) was an ancient Greek travel writer. Philo was a philosopher and writer, born about 15 B.C., who compiled an original list of the Seven Ancient Wonders and described the Temple of Artemis on page 30. The description of the Colossus of Rhodes (page 31) was written by Pliny the Younger, a Roman author who was born in A.D. 61.

INDEX

Page numbers in *italics* refer to captions and maps.

Alexander the Great 20, 46
Alexandria 5, *20*, 20–21, *21*, 25, 46, 47
    library 20–21
    lighthouse 20–21 (*see also* Pharos)
    museum 21
Antipater of Sidon 30, 46
Ark of the Covenant 22, *22*, 23
Artemis, Temple of 30, *30*, 46, 47
Aubrey holes 13
Aztecs 35

Babylon 5, *18*, 18–19
    Babel, Tower of *19*
    Gardens 18, 19 (*see also* Hanging
        Gardens)
    irrigation schemes 18, *18*
    Ishtar Gate 19
    walls 18, 30
Baths of Caracalla 33
Beaker Culture 13, 47
Borobudur 5, *42*, 42–43, *43*, 47
    pilgrimages 43, *43*
    shape 42
    stupas 43, *43*
Buddha, the 42, *42*, 43, *43*

Carnac, avenues at 5, 12, *12*, 46
Carthage 5, *28*, 28–29, 46
    cothon 28, *28*, 29
    quinqueremes *28*, 29
Central American tribes 35, 38, 39
chariot racing 18, 27, *27*, *30*, 31, 33
Cheops, Pharaoh 8, 10, *11* (*see also*
    Great Pyramid)
Chichén Itzá 5, 38–39, 46, 47
    cenotes 39, *39*
    sacred ball court 39
    temples 38, *38*, 39, *39*
Chien Chen 45, *45*
Circus Maximus *32*, 33
Colosseum 32, *32*, 46
Colossus of Rhodes 30, 31, *31*, 46, 47
Constantine Emperor 33

Deir el Bahri 9, *9*

Easter Island 5, *36*, 36–37, *37*, 46, 47
    Long Ears and Short Ears 36, 37
    statues *36*, 36–37, *37*, 46, 47
Egyptian pyramids 8, 8–9, *9*, *10*, 10–11, *11*,
    30, 46, *46*
    construction 8, *8*, 9, *9*
    tomb robbers *10*, 11

Games of Hera *27*
Great Pyramid of Cheops 8, 8–9, 30, 46,
    46
Great Serpent Mound 35, *35*

Hagia Sophia *40*, 40–41, *41*, 46, 47
    design 40, 41
Hammurabi's laws, King *18*
Hanging Gardens of Babylon 18, *18*, *19*,
    30, 46
Hebrew tribes 22–23
Hercules 26
Hisarlik 15
Holy of Holies 23
Homer 14, *15*
Hopewell mounds 5, 34, 35, *35*, 46 (*see
    also* Great Serpent Mound)

Iliad, the 14, *15*, 47
Inca Empire 35

Jericho 4, *4*, 5, 46
    walls 4, 46
Justinian, Emperor 40, *40*, 46

Knossos, Palace of 5, *16*, 16–17, *17*, 46
    bull-leaping 16, 17, *17*

Mausoleum at Halicarnassus 30, *30*, 31,
46
Maya 35, 38–39, 46
    pyramids 35
megalithic monuments 12, 13, *13*
Mentuhotpe I, Pharaoh 9, *9*, 46
Mesopotamia 6, 7, *7*, 18, 23
    cuneiform writing 7, *7*
    ziggurats 6, *6*, 7, 46
Minoan palaces 16 (*see also* Knossos)
Minos, King 16, 17
Minotaur 16

Nara 5, *44*, 44–45, 46
    Daibutsuden, the 45
    Todai-ji temple *44*, 45, 46, 47
    Toshodaiji monastery 45, *45*, 46, 47
Nazca lines 5, 34, *34*, *46*
Nebuchadnezzar II 18, 46

Olympia 5, 26–27, 46
Olympic games 26, *26*, 27, *27*, 46

Petra 5, *24*, 24–25, *25*, 46
    architecture 25
Pharos *20*, 20–21, *21*, 30, 46, 47
Phidias 27, 46
Phoenicians 22, 28, *28*, 29, 46
Pont du Gard *33*
Pyramids 6, 8–9, 10–11, 35, 38, *38* (*see
    also* Egyptian pyramids)

Rome 5, *32*, 32–33, 46
    Nero's palace 33
    Pantheon 33
    Parthenon 30, *30*

Schliemann, Heinrich 14, 15, *15*
Seven Wonders of the Ancient World 4,
    20, 26, *30*, 30–31, 46
Solomon, King 22, 23, 46
Solomon's Temple 22, 22–23, *23*, 29, 46
Sphinx, Great 10, 11, *46*
Stonehenge 5, 13, *13*, 46

Tenochtitlán 35
Teotihuacán 35
Theater at Epidaurus 30, *31*
Toltec tribe 35, 38, *38*, 39, 47
Trajan's Column 33, *33*
Troy 5, *14*, 14 15, *15*, 46
    wooden horse, the *14*, 15
Tutankhamun *10*, 11

Ur 5, 6

Valley of the Kings 11, *11*

Zeus, Statue of 26, 27, *27*, 30, 46
Zeus, Temple of 27, 46
Ziggurat 6, *6*, 7

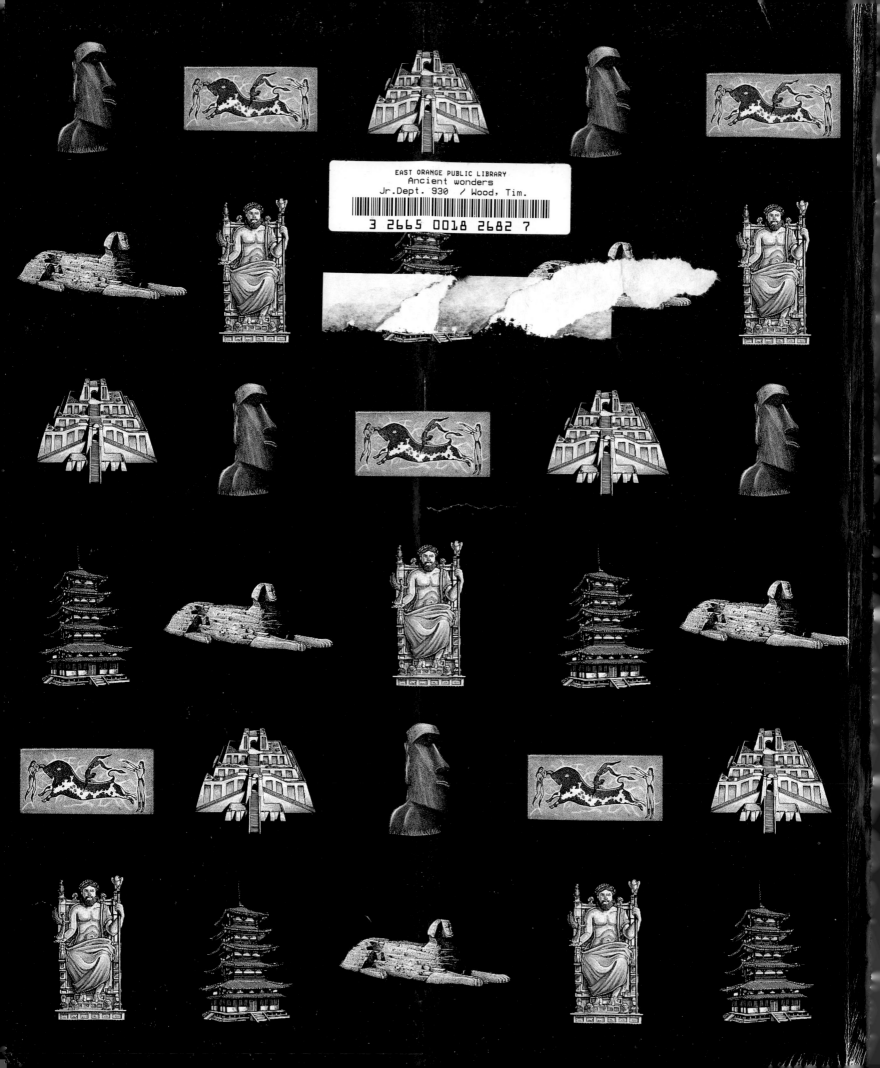